HANON'T:

Technically Speaking, Exercises for People Who Think They Should Practice More

Michael C. Wheeler

Jean Bechtel School for Music Press
Roseburg, Oregon
www.bechtelschool.com

Michael C. Wheeler
A practice space that is comfortable and accessible is equal in importance to having all necessary materials for said practice.

Introduction

The journey to becoming a competent pianist is not unlike climbing a mountain. It's difficult, it's full of challenges, and you're often left questioning why you thought it was a good idea in the first place. But you keep going, step by step, or in this case—finger by finger. Enter Hanon't: Technically Speaking, where we tackle those finger exercises we know and love from Hanon, but with one very important twist: we fix what's broken.

Let's talk about the real issues. We all know that Hanon, for all his merits, left a few things to be desired. How is it that after 38 exercises, you've never once touched a black key? Is it possible that a piano teacher could expect you to become technically proficient by ignoring half the keys on the keyboard? Yes, and here we are—ready to address that glaring oversight.

In these exercises, we'll focus on the two essentials that Hanon conveniently ignored: consistency in fingering and confronting the black keys head-on. Each exercise is crafted to address these foundational gaps—building solid habits in your finger placement while slowly introducing those tricky black keys. You'll not only build your finger independence and control, but you'll do it in a way that prepares you for the actual music you'll play, which almost certainly will require those pesky sharps and flats.

This book is for the pianist who has been battling the frustration of moving from easy scales to actual pieces, only to realize that those clean, perfectly controlled fingers from Hanon's exercises don't quite hold up when it's time to tackle something with more complexity (like, say, Chopin). **Hanon't** provides you the tools to meet these challenges head-on, making sure you don't hit a wall when it comes time to add a little bit of extra black key flavor to your practice.

So take a seat, position your hands, and prepare for a series of exercises that are designed to help you build a stronger, more complete technique—not just for show, but for the music you'll really want to play.

Franz Liszt
"Technique is the ability to translate your ideas into sound through your instrument. This is a comprehensive technique, which can only be acquired through constant practice."

Table of Contents

Feed the brain as well as the hands.

Part I, Diatonic Patterns to Get Us Started

Ludwig van Beethoven
"Art! Who comprehends her? With whom can one consult concerning this great goddess?"
– A reverent glimpse into Beethoven's view of art as something transcendent and divine.

Parallel and Contrary Diatonic Chords (Blocked)

Michael C. Wheeler

Parallel and Contrary Diatonic Chords (Broken I)

Michael C. Wheeler

Parallel and Contrary Diatonic Chords (Broken II)

Johann Wolfgang von Goethe
"A man should hear a little music, read a little poetry, and see a fine picture every day of his life."

Part II, Scale Patterns
Familiarizing Us With the Geography of the Keyboard

Clara Schumann
"There is nothing greater than the joy of making music,
but it must be earned through work."

Pentatonic Patterns Starting on White Keys

Expand to 4+ Octaves after patterns are learned

Michael C. Wheeler

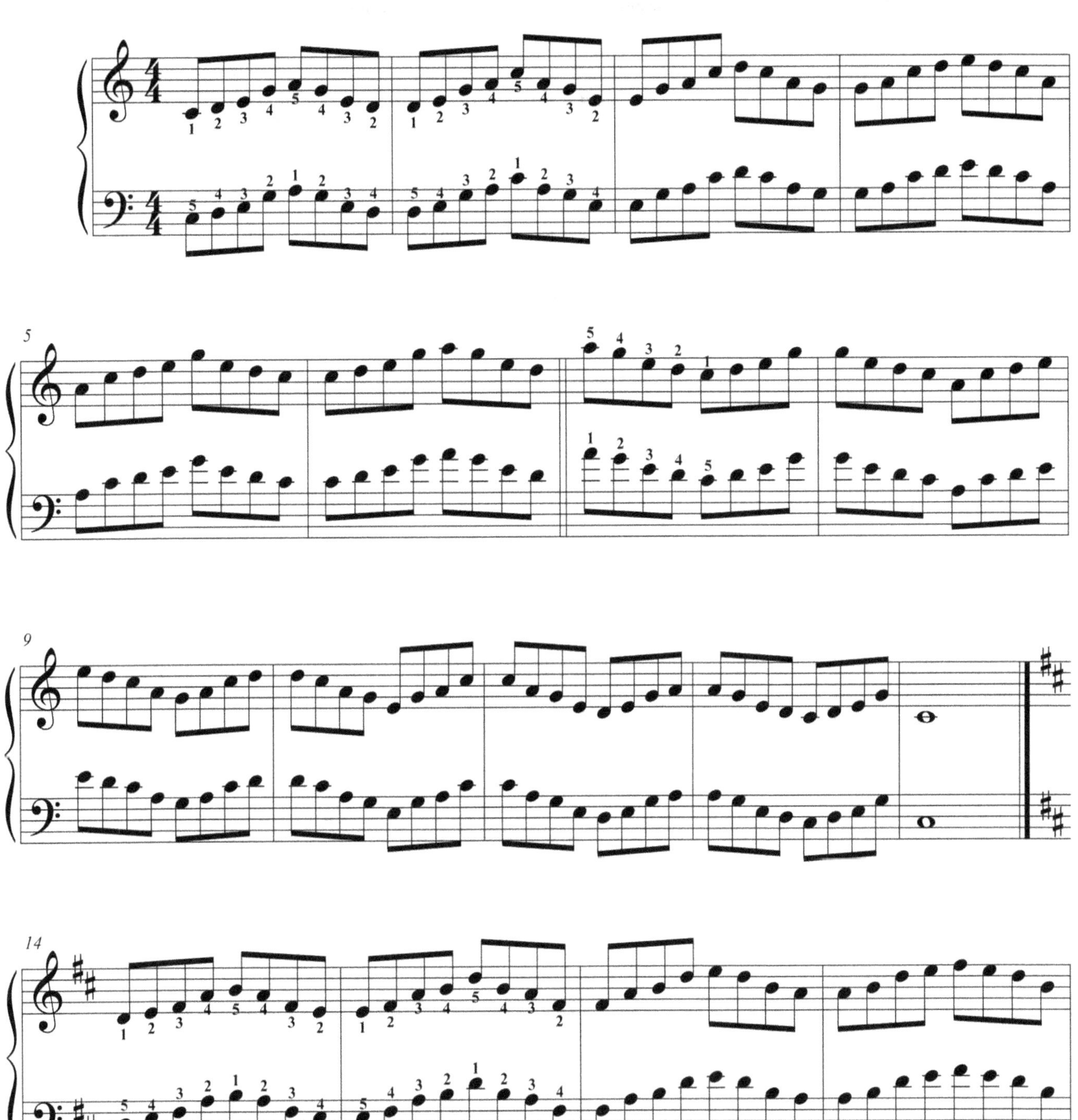

Pentatonic Patterns Starting on White Keys

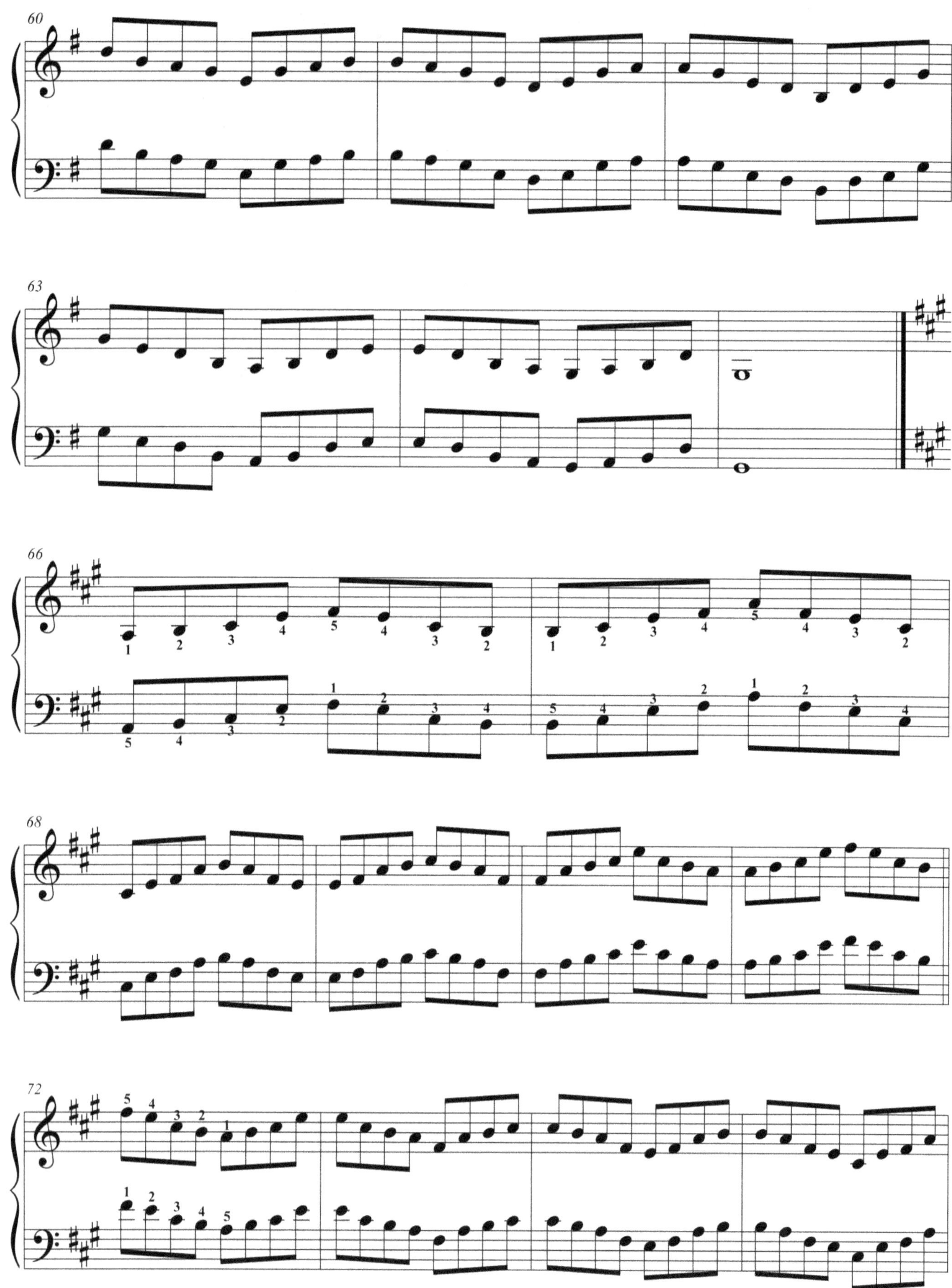

Scale Routine

To be done in keys: C, G, D, A, and E

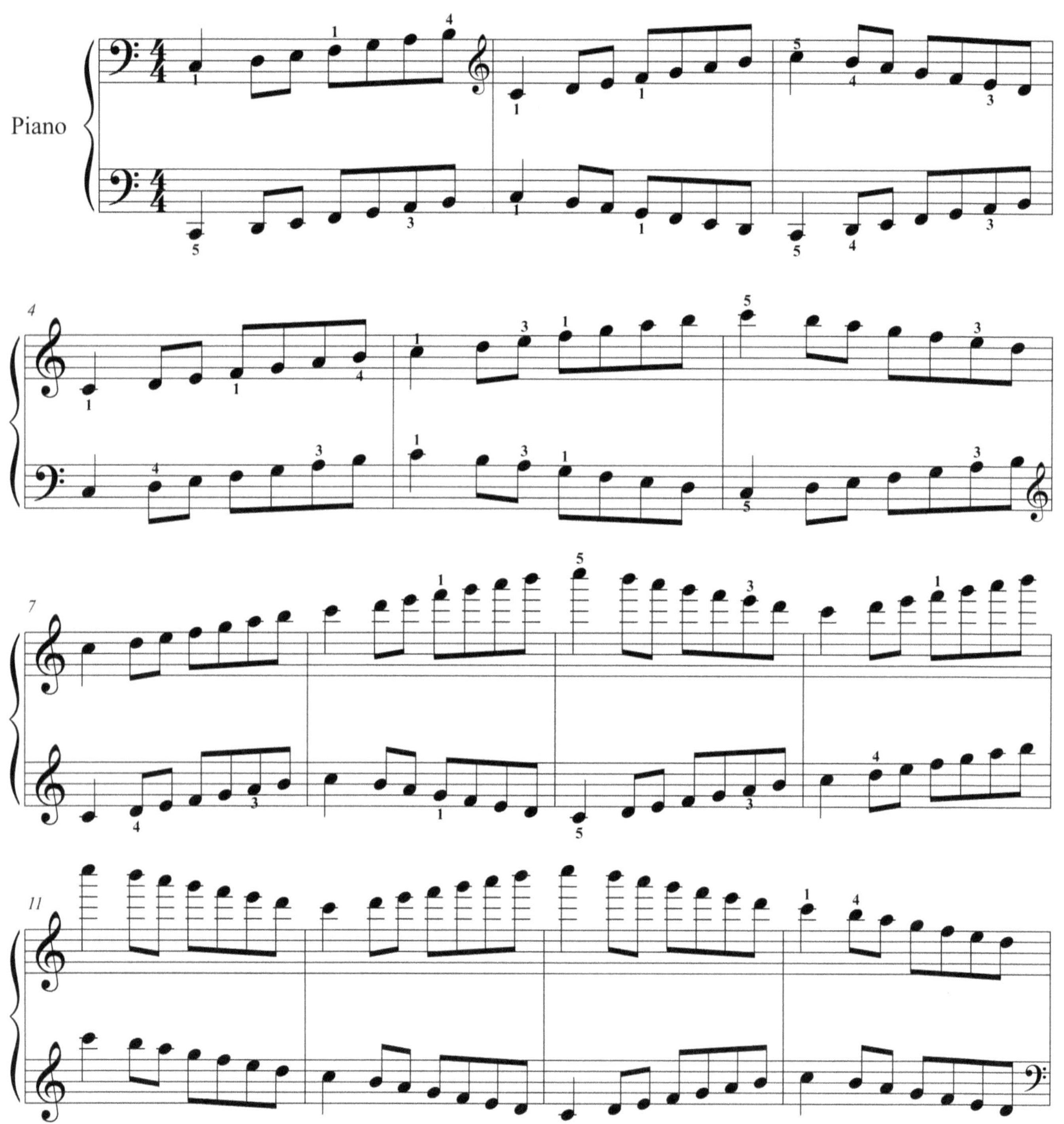

Chopin
"Simplicity is the final achievement. After one has played a
vast quantity of notes and more notes, it is simplicity that
emerges as the crowning reward of art."

Part III, Vocal Warmup Patterns
Common Vocal Technique Exercises
that Move by Half-Step

Vocal Warmup Pattern I

Every Voice Instructor Ever

Vocal Warmup Pattern II

Mitsuko Uchida
"Piano playing is much more natural than, for instance, the physical posture of playing the violin. Remember that you have the help of gravity and the hand can lie naturally on the keyboard. And remember, too, that piano-playing is not weight-lifting! If you want to play beautifully, that is the starting point – plus listening."
—Mitsuko Uchida, on the natural ergonomics of piano

Vocal Warmup in Broken Chords I

The "mum" and "no" Exercise

Some voice teacher a long time ago

© Jean Bechtel School for Music Press
www.bechtelschool.com

Vocal Warmup in Broken Chords I

Vocal Warmup in Broken Chords II

The Rossini Scale*

Rossini, I Think

*pleay one octave higher for female vocalists

Vocal Warmup in Broken Chords II

Johann Sebastian Bach
"There's nothing remarkable about it. All one has to do is hit
the right keys at the right time and the instrument plays itself."

Part IV, Accompaniment Patterns
For Students Playing in Popular Styles of Music Who Need to Do Simple Chord Accompaniments

Alfred Cortot
"The main thing is not to practice a passage until you get it
right—but to practice it until you can't get it wrong."

Typical Piano Accompaniment Patterns

To be used with any chord progression(s) of the student's choice

Rosina Lhévinne (1880–1976)
"Piano playing is a physical art with great traditions
behind it. Its literature is a treasure trove, waiting for
exploration and enjoyment."

Part V, Hand Extension Exercises
For People With Full-Grown Hands

Artur Rubinstein
"If I don't practice one day, I know it. If I don't practice
two days, the critics know it. If I don't practice three
days, the public knows it."

Hand Extension Exercise I
Fully Diminished Chord

Hand Extension Exercise II
Minor Seventh Chords

Hand Extension Exercise III
Major Seventh Chords

Rosina Lhévinne
"By intense concentration, love of your work, and the
spirit in which you approach it, you can do more in a half
hour than in an hour spent purposelessly."

Part VI, All 12 Major/Minor Chords

All Twelve Major Chords

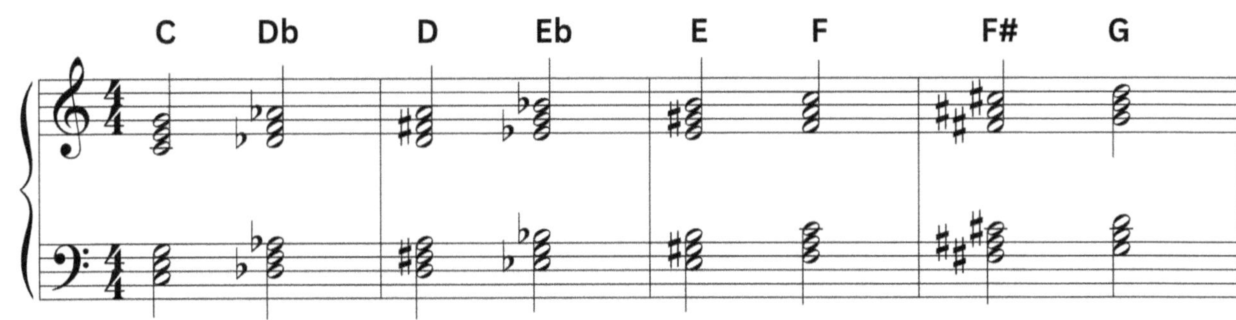

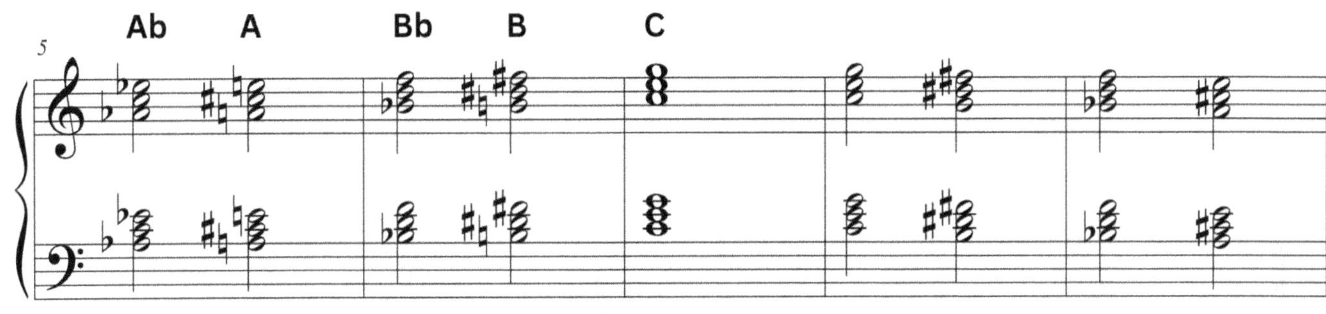

Marie Jaëll (1846–1925)
"The intelligence of the hand must be cultivated alongside the intelligence of the mind."
Marie Jaëll, a French pianist and pedagogue, integrated neuroscience into her teaching, advocating for a holistic approach to piano technique that combines mental and physical

All Twelve Minor Chords

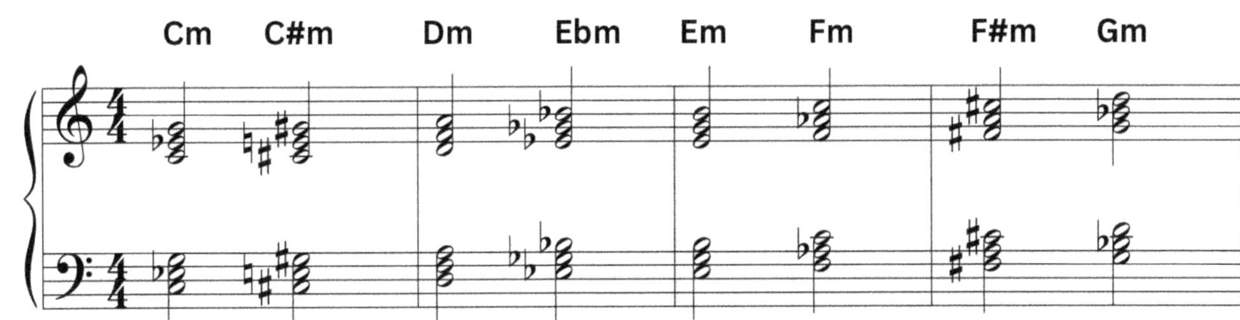

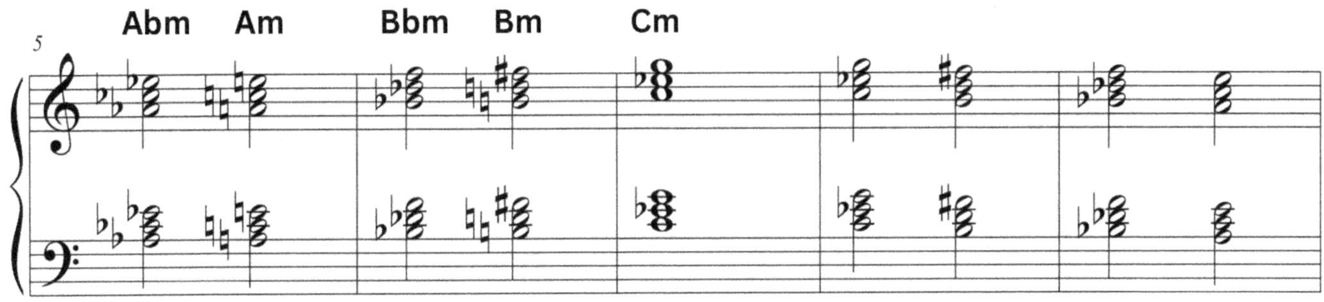

Carl Czerny
"The fingers must become so skillful that they instinctively strike the correct keys without the slightest thought from the brain."

Part VI, Chromatic Exercises

Fanny Hensel (1805–1847)
"Music is a language that speaks to the soul; practice is the
grammar that makes fluency possible."
Fanny Hensel, a gifted pianist and composer, highlighted the
necessity of practice in mastering the expressive language of music.

Chromatic Exercise I

Chromatic Exercise II

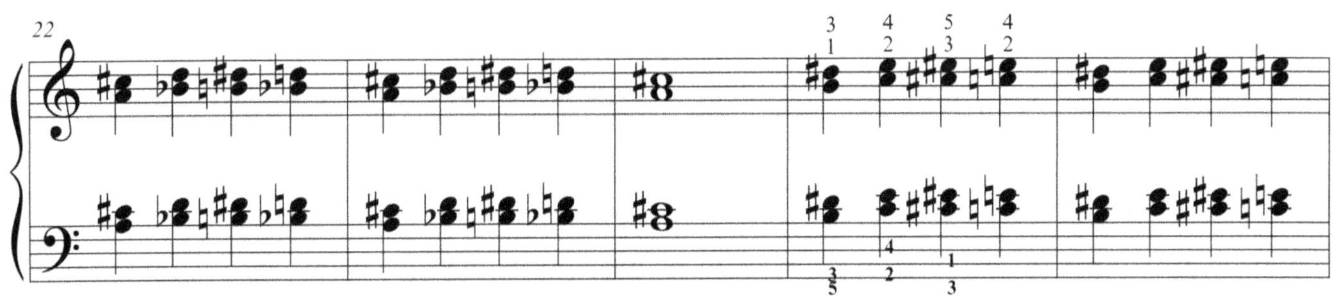

Chromatic Exercise III

Amy Beach (1867–1944)
"Technique is the servant of expression; without it, the soul cannot speak through music."
Amy Beach, an American composer and pianist, believed that technical proficiency is essential for conveying emotional depth in performance.

Chromatic Exercise IV

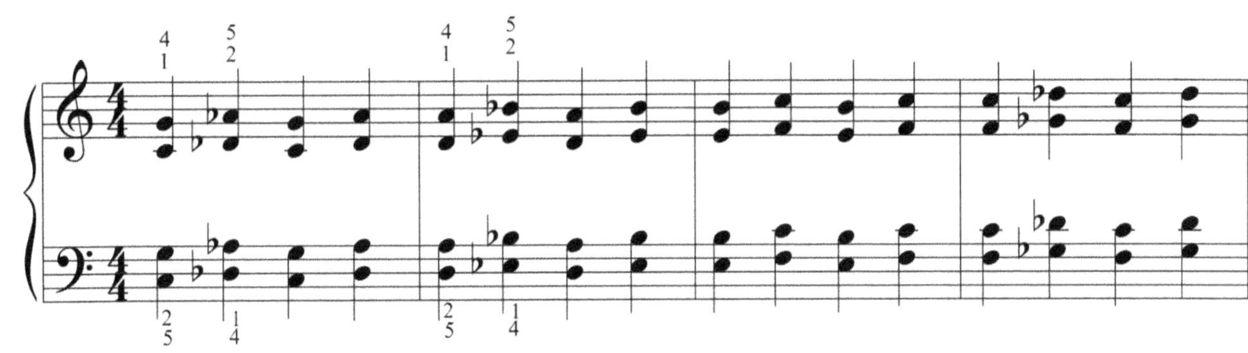

Chromatic Octave Exercise I

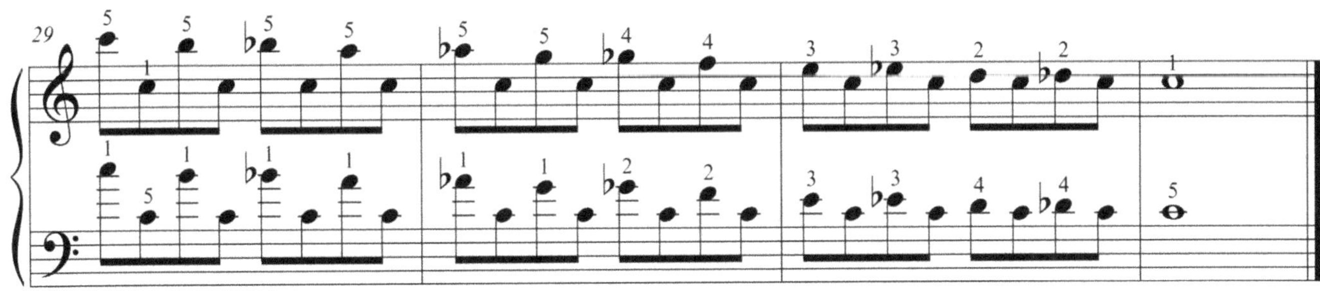

Chromatic Octave Exercise II

Nina Simone (1933–2003)
"Once I understood Bach's music, I wanted to be a concert pianist. Bach made me dedicate my life to music, and it was that teacher who introduced me to his world."

Part VII,
More (Difficult) Scale patterns

Scale Pattern I

Indicated Fingering is a Suggestion Only

Scale Pattern I

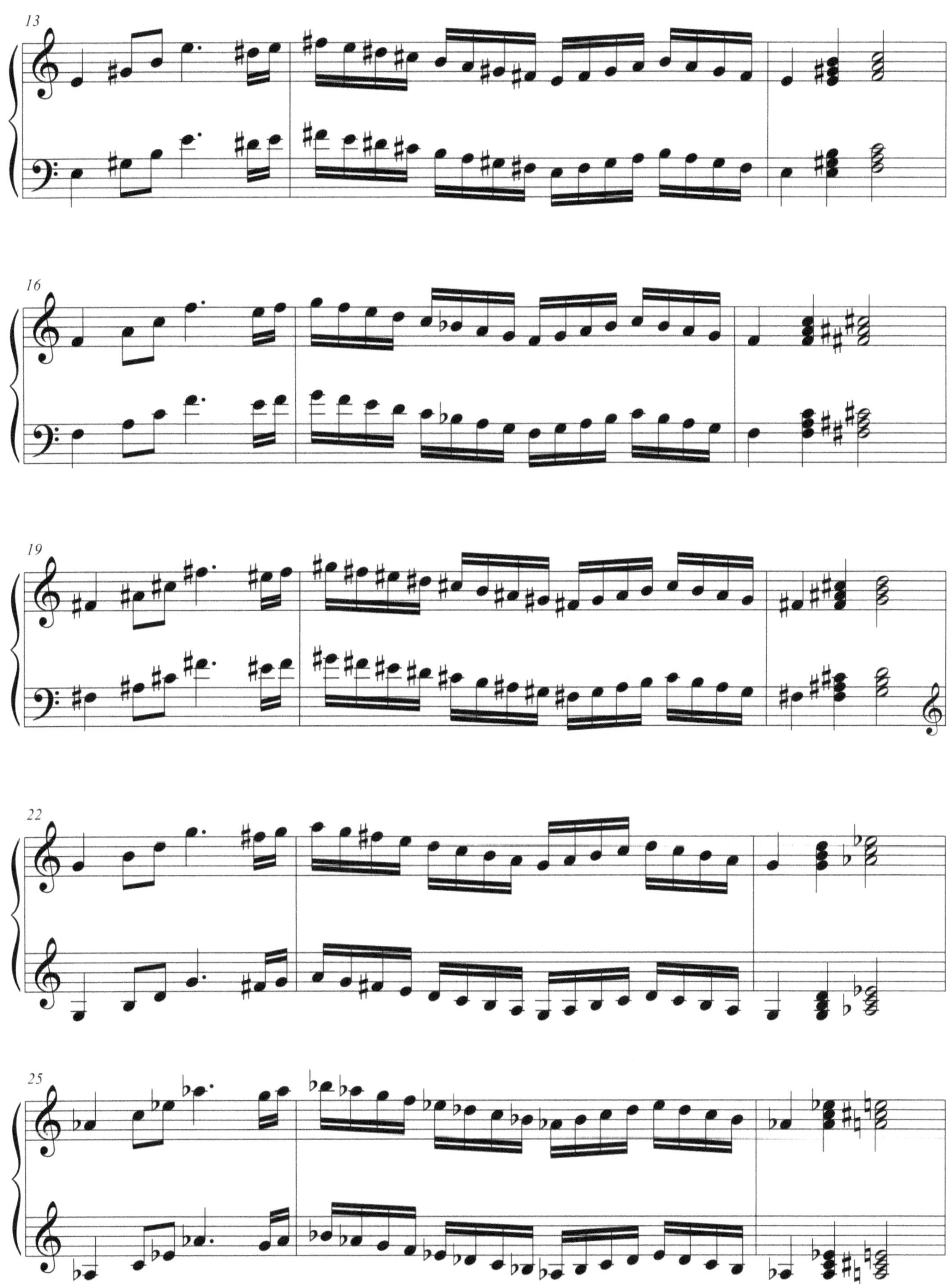

Robert Schumann (1810–1856)
"You must get to the point where you can say anything you like with your hands and always with the same ease."
Schumann saw technical fluency not as the goal but as the means to express deeper musical ideas.

Scale Pattern III

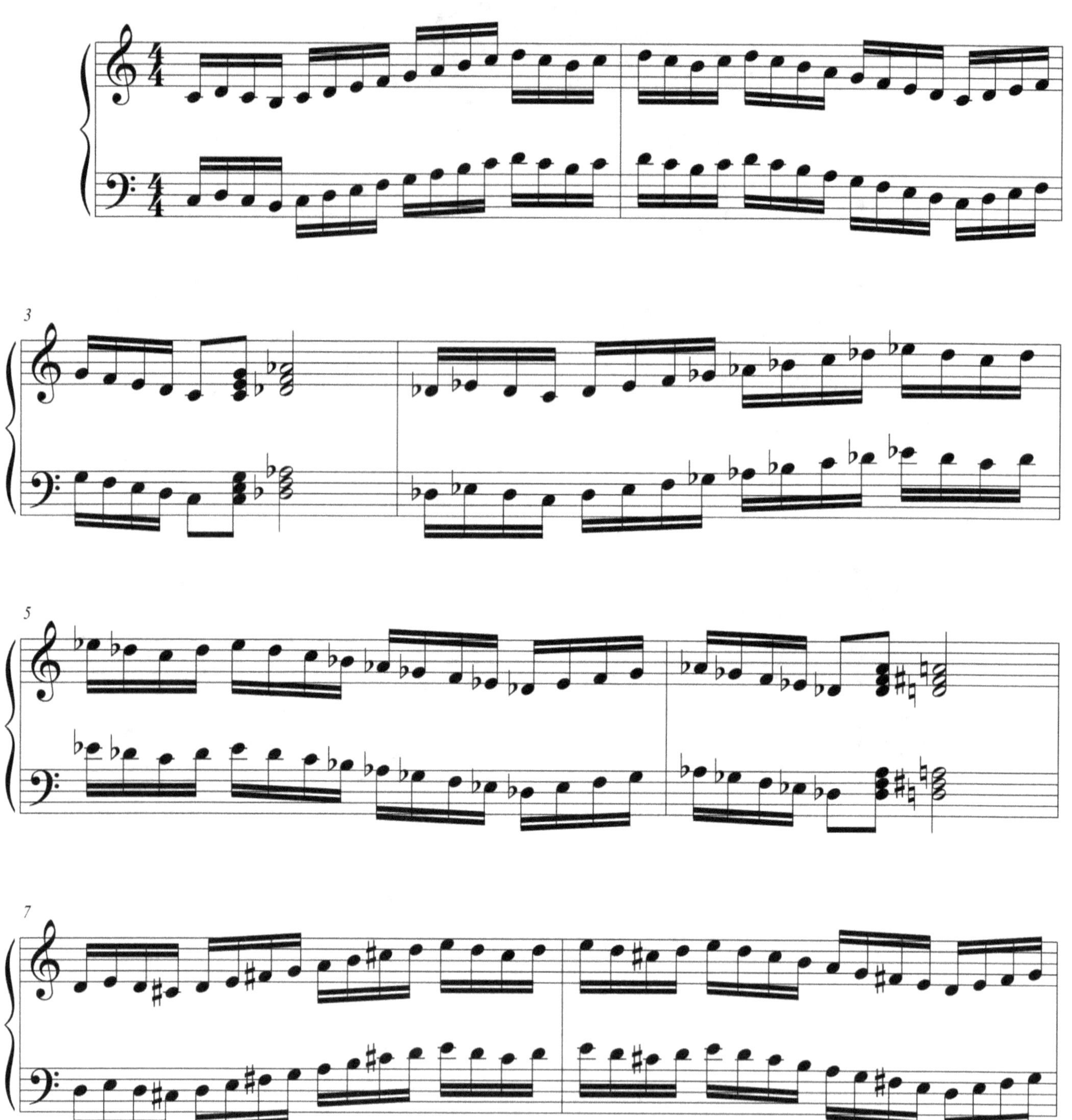

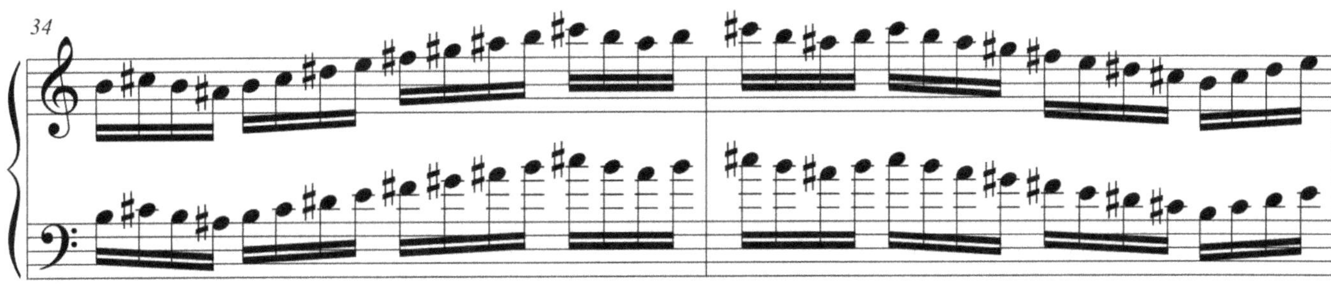

Carl Czerny (1791–1857)
"Speed and clarity should not be achieved through force, but through understanding and economy of motion."

Whole Tone Scales

www.ingramcontent.com/pod-product-compliance
Lightning Source LLC
LaVergne TN
LVHW081640220726
843527LV00037B/543